The Story of
Christmas

The Story of Christmas

Told in pictures by
Margaret W. Tarrant

and in simple words by
Katharine B. Bamfield

LONDON: THE MEDICI SOCIETY LTD.

NEW EDITION © 1996
including new reproductions from the original paintings

PRINTED IN ENGLAND
ISBN 0 85503 011 9

The Story of Christmas

God's Promise of a Saviour

THE BIBLE tells us that in the Beginning GOD created Man in His own Image. But very soon men and women began to do the things GOD had told them not to do, and with their disobedience sin came into the beautiful world that GOD had made. GOD was very sorry and He pitied mankind and made a promise that in His own time He would send a Saviour to help them.

For hundreds of years GOD'S people wondered when His promise was coming true, for all the time the hope of a Messiah or Deliverer was kept alive in their hearts by the Prophets who were teachers chosen by GOD. But most people were looking for a powerful earthly King, who would lead his armies into battle and make their nation free and great.

At last, at GOD'S appointed hour, an Angel— GABRIEL who stands in the presence of GOD— was sent to earth to carry the joyful news that the Time had come, the promised Deliverer was to be born, as the Prophets had foretold.

Now the Angel's message was not given to a Princess or a great lady, but he was sent to Nazareth in Galilee to Mary, a humble Jewish maiden, who was about to marry Joseph, the carpenter. But though Joseph was only a carpenter by trade, the great King David was his ancestor, and prophets and psalmists of old had all pointed to the promise that

the coming Messiah or Saviour should be of the royal line of David.

Mary was overcome by the Angel's tidings—that she was to be the Mother of the Holy One, the Son of GOD. But she answered the call in simple and humble obedience.

Gabriel had also spoken to Mary of her cousin Elizabeth, for she too was to be the mother of a promised son, known to us as St. John the Baptist. He was to prepare the way for one greater than himself—even Mary's own Son.

So Mary set out to visit Elizabeth in her home among the hills, and to ask her advice.

Just before the time came for Mary's babe to be born into the world, the Roman Emperor ordered all his Jewish subjects to report at the place where they belonged, so that his officers might count the number of the people. So Joseph and Mary had to set out for Bethlehem, the City of David, the very place where the Prophets had said the Messiah should be born.

There were great crowds moving about, for many were travelling because of this census or counting

of the people, and when Joseph and Mary got to Bethlehem the Inn was full. So they had to shelter in the stable, and there, in that humble place, Mary's Babe was born. He was the Heavenly King, the Son of GOD, but He had no earthly palace, not even a real bed, and His mother laid Him to sleep in a manger.

Men did not know who had come to live among them, but the Angels were watching, and they told

the wonderful news to some simple Shepherds, as they guarded their sheep in the fields that night.

And the rejoicing of Heaven overflowed unto earth as the Angel hosts sang together "Glory to GOD in the Highest and on earth Peace, Goodwill towards men."

Then the Shepherds thought they would go and see their new-born Saviour for themselves, for had not the Angel said "Unto you is born a Saviour"? And they left their flocks and walked to Bethlehem as fast as they could in the night.

When they got to Bethlehem they found it was all true, just as the Angel had told them. There was the new-born Babe and His Mother and Joseph. And the Baby was lying in the manger that held hay for the oxen to eat. But the Shepherds knew this was no ordinary infant. And they worshipped Him.

Eight days after His birth

the baby Boy received His Name,

as an Angel had foretold to Joseph.

Note that Name and what it means.

JESUS—

"for He shall save His people from their sins."

The Presentation in the Temple

Later on, forty days from His birth, Mary and Joseph took Him to the Temple to be presented and dedicated to the Lord, and there a wonderful thing happened. A very old and holy man named Simeon had been assured by the Holy Spirit that he should see "the Lord's Christ" before he died. Coming into the Temple just then he felt that this promise to him was being fulfilled. Taking the Child in his arms,

he knew that here lay the Saviour, not only of Israel, but of the whole world.

"Mine eyes have seen Thy Salvation, which Thou hast prepared before the face of all people," sang Simeon, and his words still ring out in Christian worship every day at evening.

There was an aged widow, too, one Anna, who lived in the Temple, and she too joined the happy group round the infant Jesus, and she with them gave thanks to God and proclaimed the Babe as the Redeemer.

The Three Wise Men

Then appeared three magnificent figures—Wise Men (or Magi) from the East. They were learned men, who studied the stars, and they had seen a new star, a royal star—the sign of a King—appear in the eastern sky. Guided by its light they set out on a long journey to find this new monarch, whoever he might be, to worship him.

The star pointed to Jerusalem, and when they arrived there they enquired of King Herod, where the new King was to be born and where they could find him. "At Bethlehem" answered the priests

and teachers, who knew what was written in the sacred books.

And at Bethlehem, still led by the Star, the Magi found the infant King. (By this time the holy Family had moved into a house, and the little Lord Jesus no longer lay in a manger). The travellers entered into His presence and fell down and worshipped Him. Then they opened the treasures they had brought and laid them at His feet.

The gifts that St. Matthew's gospel mentions have, no doubt, a spiritual meaning. They offered Gold to Him as King, with Frankincense they worshipped Him, and they laid bitter Myrrh before Him in token of His sufferings yet to come.

When the Magi had enquired of King Herod about this new king and where he was to be found, Herod pretended that he too wished to pay homage to the unknown monarch, but really he was jealous at the idea of a rival, and made up his mind to kill him. So to make sure that the royal Child should not survive, he gave the cruel order that all boy babies up to two years old in and around Bethlehem should be destroyed.

The Wise Men did not visit Herod again, as he had asked them to do, for GOD gave them warning in a dream, and they returned to their own country by another way.

The infant Lord Jesus was not among the poor babes (the Holy Innocents, we call them) who were slain by Herod's cruelty. An Angel warned Joseph in a dream of Herod's wicked intention and told him to take Mary and the holy Child and to escape into the land of Egypt.

They stayed in Egypt as long as Herod lived, and when they returned to their own country, it was in Nazareth that they settled, a safer spot than

Bethlehem, as Herod's son was reigning in his father's place.

And the name of Nazareth is for ever sacred to us, as it was the home of the Lord Jesus in His boyhood.

There Joseph the carpenter had his workshop. There Jesus "wrought with Joseph with chisel, saw and plane." In that home He was "subject to

His parents" and obeyed them, and there He "increased in wisdom and stature and in favour with GOD and man."

The story of Christmas is ended. But it never grows stale or out-of-date. To all who hold out loving hands of welcome to the Christ Child, and kneel at His cradle, He bestows a gift that lasts for ever—even a share in His own divine eternal Life.